KAL EIDO SCOPE

Maddison Woods

KALEIDOSCOPE

Maddison Woods

Gubbi Gubbi Country
Australia

Copyright © 2024 Maddison Woods

All rights reserved. No part of this book may be reprinted or reproduced or utilised in any form or by any electronic, mechanical, or other means, now known or hereafter invented, including photocopying and recording, or in any information storage or retrieval system, without permission in writing from the publisher.

Paperback 978-0-6459852-7-6

Cover and internal illustrations by Maddison Woods

Editor
Emma Mitchell

Marketing & publishing support
Pooja Kumar
Sarah Bradbury
Michelle Bùi Hoàng

Typeset & cover design
Wallea Eaglehawk

First published in 2024

Moonrise
Gubbi Gubbi Country, Australia
www.moonrise.revolutionaries.com.au

Contents

Introduction	x
Meraki	1
The Song of Ostara	4
Dawn	13
Daffodils	14
The Letter	17
Rebirth	19
How small we must appear to the hummingbird	21
Mo shíorghrá (My beloved)	22
The Dancer - 1	23
Hungry for Happiness	25
We were wicked	27
Komorebi	29
Dormiveglia	30
The Song of Litha	33
Multitudinous Incarnadine	51
Mångata	53
The Prayer	55

Ocean Blue	57
Student of Life	60
Fragrance	74
Horizon	75
Shelter	77
Midnight Sun	78
Summerland	79
Murr-ma	81
The Snake and the Spider	83
Ocean Beds	87
Leap Year	89
The Song of Mabon	90
The Rolling Fields of Sorghum	93
Virago	95
Alyssum	96
A ribcage full of roses	97
Verve	99
The Dancer – 2	103
Lungs	105
Hawk	107
Dies Irae	108
Purple Hyacinths	109
Gloaming	113
Whitman's sole	114

The Song of Yule	115
Coffee	121
Everywhere	122
The Skimming Stone	123
How brightly shine the stars of yonder!	125
I walked down the path of art	127
Girl with Goldfish	128
Woolf Street	129
Inheritance	131
52	133
Ship of Theseus	135
Ouroboros	136
Love-Lies-Bleeding	137
Soup	139
Ammil	140
Innsæi	141
Revolution	143
This Kingdom	145

Introduction

I contemplate the irony of contemplating on the words of those who have devoted their lives to contemplation. I contemplate on the liminal, not linear, progression of thoughts; their jagged, scribbled nature. I shall write as such. And as I contemplate on the contemplations of those devoted to contemplating, I, too, make myself a wallflower, a cloud, a wind-swept leaf: become an observer, an invisible eye, a walking mirror; relinquish upon myself a life of reflection and meditation; a voyeur of nature and its divine presence. Pen and paper, my only tools, accompany my only earthly gift. Energy of tongue and mind of business, I do not possess. Numbers and the conversations of others elude me. All I own is what I see, what I hear, taste, smell, feel, and the blessed ability to write. I do so, as though any day I may wake to find myself a mute, or completely stripped of all my senses. So, with irony pushed aside, I endeavour to pursue a life of study, of contemplation...preserve what may be a small piece of comfort and blissful solitude through the words of a quiet, but hopeful, romantic.

Meraki

Be gentle;

Every poem, a bloom picked
From this inner Garden,
Presented to you with the fragility of petals
And the stubbornness of thorns.
Every bloom, a doorway,
An escape created within me,
Melded out of magic,
Suspended in a moment,
Pressed and dried, and sent to you.

Welcome to my Garden.

The Song of Ostara

It is a universal craving; a delight—
The feeling of waking well-rested,
Full of the same energy
        that encourages the birds to sing,
        the flowers to grow,
        and all living beings embrace
        the outside world.
The buzz of life in Spring is full of youth;
        playful and charming,
        and everything around you appears
        a few shades brighter.

The art, the natural beauty,
        is so enchanting.
All those colours Mother Earth employs,
Her whole palette on display;
        both sights and smells.
That is just to the human eye!
Ultraviolet, the vision of the bee—
Even the plainest of flowers
        is a visual masterpiece.

Comfort comes more readily,
In new forms,
As we pack away our heaters,
Our heavy coats and blankets.
It is the season to feel young again
  and put your bare feet in the grass,
  watch as a new world emerges
  from beneath the soil.
To take in fresh air
  and fall in love with life.

I gather vases of pink tulips
With sprigs of lavender
And adorn every windowsill;
The sunlight catching the petals
  and casting a faint blush of colour
  around the room.
How can you not believe in magic?
Especially in the presence of flowers;
As even the darkest room
  is brightened in their company.
The stem and the petals
Do not discriminate.

All their pretty smiles
        are for everyone.

Can you hear it?
Listen closely, not with your ears
But your heart.
Golden trumpets call in this new phase.
'Spring is here!' they cry,
Wave their heads in greeting.
They will tell you stories of the earth,
        of hardships and growth,
        if you choose to listen.
This is their calling,
The purpose of their form—
So, sit in the grassy pews
And listen close
As the daffodils tell their tale.

So much symmetry spirals
        within the face of a dahlia,
Or unfurls with each petal of a rose.
Colours collide with their closeness,
Yet there is still so much harmony
        within this abundant garden.

No one tells red daisies
> not to grow next to pink snapdragons,
Or that the gerbera and the foxglove
> do not look beautiful in each other's
> company.
They grow and bloom
> in all shapes, sizes and colours,
This great mosaic of Nature,
And all of it is good.

Spring belongs to the winged creatures.
Oh, how I envy these energetic
> and hard-working creatures of the Earth!
Would life be more peaceful
> if humans had wings?
Real wings, stretching in unison
> with our shoulders, our arms.
What would they be made of?
Transparent, like the bee and the dragonfly?
Soft, like the butterfly and the moth?
Or strong and feathered, like a bird;
> These angels of earth, blessed to ride the
> winds
> great distances, to travel the world

with absolute freedom.

I try to keep a piece of Spring with me,
All year,
Everywhere I go.
A pop of colour;
A photograph—an everlasting capture
    of the inevitably fleeting foliage;
These words imbued with the senses,
    the gentle breeze that plays with my hair,
    the warmth that matches my own body
    heat.
Poetry to trigger (happily) the
    delicious and tantalising
    scents, sounds and sights.

There is no shame in admiring
    the beauty of things you do not understand.
If you observe something to be beautiful,
It does not need explanation.
When beauty needs a reason,
    then all beautiful things disappear.
As we venture further into
    the natural world,

>we are humbled by just how plain
>we are as humans.

See all things as beautiful,
For we have no grounds on which to judge.

Why do we call the space between leaves
>'negative space'?

I see unique windows in various shades of green,
Framing the blue sky and
>the world around them.

A new perspective,
Full of movement and ever-changing visions.
There is always something to be seen
>in those seemingly empty spaces.

Be gentle as the sensitive souls emerge.
Their hidden strengths lie elsewhere.
Let them be, like the calm river
That, over time, cuts through stone.

We are surrounded by spirits that can grow
>to impossible heights.

Walk into the forest,

Stand at the base of the tallest tree
And look up.

Day and night in equilibrium.
The scales of energy hang flush,
The planet sits up straight
And all things exist within the balance.
Great fortune falls upon the southern hemisphere
As the cusp of the woman and the scales
Falls upon this great equinox.

Conversations with creatures of my own species
        are of no interest to me.
Although I understand what they say,
Their words groan under the collective weight
        of human importance.
Language is far greater than a sound
        or a written word;
I marvel at the thought of all those mysterious
        and unheard languages.
Perhaps there is a language entirely dependant
        on the subtle combination of muscle fibre
        twitches,
        or the rising and falling heat in our skin.

I prefer conversations with babbling creeks
And common stones, wise with age.
With the spider, as I compliment it on its skills
       as a natural engineer
       and the genius of its web.
To speak smooth and comforting words
To the moth, or the skink
As you gently release it outside.
Animism;
Conversations exchanged in a glance or a touch.
Every inner thought heard,
       every inner feeling felt.
The peace of being alone, but never lonely.

See how quickly the newborns adapt and grow!
Even the smallest and the slowest snail
As it seeks shade and sustenance,
Naturally holds within instincts
       we could never dream of,
       and skills we take decades to learn.
The wisteria learns to climb,
And the chick learns to fly
Before a newborn child can properly gaze
       into the eyes of their mother.

The prayers of seeds I scattered in the late Summer
Took root in Autumn,
Waited in Winter,
Then were granted in a glorious flourish.
All things have their time;
Butterflies, flowers and prayers.
We do not rush the orchid to bloom,
Nor the maple tree to grow,
Nor the stars to shoot across the midnight sky.
Patience is the greatest lesson taught
In Nature's vast classroom.

I imagine the Universe to be a small thing;
Planets and stars float around
       like cells under a microscope.
Are we merely germs of the cosmos?
Are we, in fact, contained within
       a dew drop on the petal
       of a small flower
       plucked by a being of indescribable form?

Dawn

The trees all speak in whispers,
Their voices sail on Spring breezes;
I hear them shudder,
        and shake,
        and shrug off the shawl of Winter white.
They whisper and yawn themselves awake,
        and wish upon the winds to wear
        the most wonderful emerald coat.
And I watch, waiting, in the warming western winds,
        to see the shooting buds of Spring
        and the sight of the unfurling shade.

Daffodils

Spring meadows of soft Sun,
Grass of silk sways silver-green waves,
Whip around waking blooms;
A heavenly sight, an ocean bright
With golden trumpets to hail the season.
Through an earth hard and cold,
Resilient;
Admiration of the decadent growth,
I gaze upon the golden gathering,
A floral heaven of fleeting foliage,
Forever bound to a wicked world
With only the Sun to see—
And I see a sea of sunlight,
For the Sun must look down
And perceive them to be
His very own reflection.

The Letter

Love; you have many acquaintances,
and of you I have heard so much.
It is as though you have shaken hands
        with the whole world.
When will I know you?
I feel as if I am a child,
        on the cusp of reality,
        writing my final letter to Santa.
Although your name is dipped in pleasure
        and spread like candlelight,
some have described your presence as pain;
Is that Cupid's arrow hitting its mark?
Or is such a sensation temporary,
        and you have come to take back
        your property
        with a swift, cutting pull?
The barb of a stingray.
Alas, I know nothing
        but what I can imagine,
        which is very little,
        and I pay no attention to the critique of
        others.

Shall we meet? New acquaintances, at this age?
I do not know you, therefore I do not miss you,
>   like the others.
Perhaps knowing you, for the first time, at this age,
when my heart is no longer flexible,
would cause too much pain—
And you might kill me.

Rebirth

After a great rain
The lake looks like smooth, glossy turquoise;
Slides softly into a mirror of the sky—midday; dusk;
At night, two moons on display
And the world wrapped in stars;
Space and Earth collide,
        Reflect each other...
The wind grazes the water's surface,
It's only chance to touch the moon...
I step out into the lake
And standing still, imagine
The great celestial body an egg in the water,
        And I break through—a cosmic child,
Born again in a different light,
To see Life through the eyes of the Milky Way.

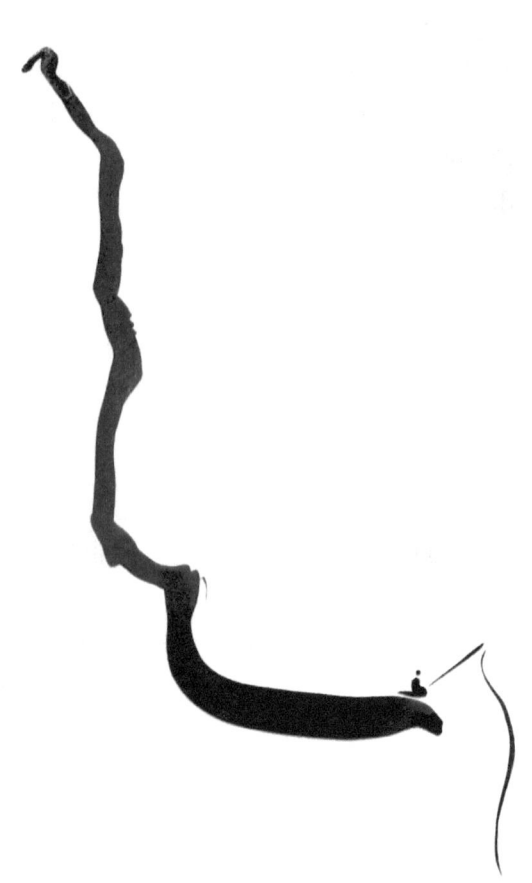

How small we must appear to the hummingbird

How small we must appear to the hummingbird
As it searches for its next meal;
We, who believe ourselves as big as
        the mountains—miniscule
Next to the sweet, life-giving nectar of the flower.
With such colourful faces upon the earth,
How can we perceive ourselves as anything
        other than their servants?
Our bland flesh that attracts none;
We should bow to the rainbow land that
        seeks to sustain us all.

Mo shíorghrá (My beloved)

Mo shíorghrá,

Gift me signs of your coming;
Butterflies in groups of three, petals
Floating down a murky stream, Twilight at the
midday hour.
Roaming; through time and decay,
Captured glimpses of possibility
In sunbeams and blades of grass,
Fragile; a communion of souls
Untouched—I have faith;
A belief never once had but felt
In bones and waters, and caressed
By winds across shoulder-blades,
That somewhere,
Beyond distance and face,
Over the chasm of age and flesh,

There you are.

The Dancer – 1

In a park, I watch a young woman
> dance beneath a Flame tree,

As passers-by declare her insanity...
But I think she looks beautiful and free,
> moving improvised, delicately.

If to move with our whole being
> is so to be judged as crazy,

Then I, too, wish to be induced into mania...
How often do we move? Truly move,
> beyond walking and exercise—

To stretch our limbs and sway as branches,
To twist and glide as birds do,
To feel our ribs expand and our hearts
> open—breathe ever deeper...

I pity us all, this rejection of free
> movement; of expression;

With what have we bound ourselves as
> invisible straitjackets?

Not even in venues of dance does movement
> flow free and unapologetically...

To dance is to surrender to the motions
> of true nature—

Ah! Surrender. There it is, our stubborn shackle;
We do not wish to appear less than 'perfect'...
I beg you, relinquish some control,
        or we may all turn to stone.

Hungry for Happiness

Creativity is play; an appetite;
It is a challenge, to explore opposites –
So, I cover my darkness
        in rainbow lights.
The length of my sadness
shall be a flash fiction
in the hefty novel of my being.
My self-concept is erratic,
the constantly changing fragments
of a kaleidoscope.
Happiness, I shall fear no longer.

I do not want to be the tragic, suffering artist.
I will not be a faded flower.

We were wicked

We were wicked;
Such a cruel delight in which we bathed, and
Behaved as an immortal might.
A broken, beastly bacchanal, a feast on lonely souls,
And quenched our thirst on sacred earth—
A rare and richly tended soil.
Through empty eyes of the lost,
Rivers of Time gone past will run,
And from the skulls of victors shall we drink until we're done.
We were wicked;
Whipping lashes at a mountain range,
'Til it calls evil our own name,
For we wish our names heard on the winds,
And whispered in the Hall of Sins:
Fearsome and untouchable.

Komorebi

A glittering of dust does fall,
Combine with dew drops to christen
The path of a new day.
Streaming tunnels of light
Do feed Earth with Sun's nectar;
Crowns the trees in honey-glow,
Yet in the shade does fragile fungi feast,
And the halls of the forest palace
Brim with servants of Her kingdom.
Ribboned streams like diamonds glisten,
Sing with branches humming choir,
And Sun rains upon Her reign in rejoice,
Adorned Her with golden jewels.

Dormiveglia

Suspended,

A weightless moment hangs between morning rays,
Visions of orange swirl behind closed eyelids,
Hypnotic hum of breath and human activity
Beyond dreams and duvets,
A comfortable pull of light against eyelashes, Body
warmth, perfect and pleasant,
And dreams still play within
In vivid technicolour.

Suspended,

Betwixt to safe spaces, and
Imprinted upon pillow cases and puffy cheeks,
Sunshine and alarm clocks,
Between both comfort and disbelief, A tempestuous
knowing that,
For a solitary second,
Sleep and consciousness coexist In perpetual
synchronicity.

The Song of Litha

The months of Summer are not
        scattered throughout the year,
They blend into one Being;
Southernly, they tie together all the years,
Too, sewing Time into one Being—
A vast timeline stitched by the Sun:
The Beginning and the End.

There is no greater artist;
Mother Earth creates electric skies so blue,
I feel as though the world is a painting,
every colour used.
Or perhaps a diorama—
a small box of reality…
Should I walk far enough, shall I come to a sudden stop?

To sit comfortably on a blanket on the grass,
And listen to simple pleasures—
A world about me and without me:
The magpie shaking seeds from trees…
Trees swaying to the wind-song…

The butterfly dancing in its final hours...
The solitary sound of footsteps as
        a silent wanderer secretly worships the sun...
And I, another solitary soul,
Slow down time and observe...

I gaze upon a pond and see it full of life—
An intertwined flow;
A concoction of energies: bird, fish and grass,
Weave as spirals, yet never collide;
And I see collective peace,
Reflected in the teal shimmer on a brown duck's wing.

Colour belongs not just to the Spring,
But to all seasons in a variety of hues:
The crystal white of Winter, its snow and naked trees...
The warm glow of Autumn, with its ever-changing leaves
        and a reminder to breathe...
Summer is purple, to me;
Streets showered in the soft petals of Jacaranda trees,
And the watercolour wash of a lavender dusk.

The skeletal black of the Ibis head:
A death mask scavenging through
        rubbish and decay;
A humble reminder in this fragile season
        of blossoming existence.
Earth's Great Wheel.

I breathe in the trees
As they breathe in me;
This ancient relationship of life.
I honour the trees imbued with years
        and knowledge I shall never possess.
I chase away mental darkness
By looking towards the heavens,
Beneath the canopy of trees with halos of light;
And towards the ground,
An ecosystem too great to count
        or understand.

Great Sunflowers, Queens of the garden,
Watch over all as guardians;
I perceive them to be the eyes of the Sun...
        Follow the light...
Impart to me your wisdom so I, too,

        may follow the Sun.
I scatter your seeds as offerings and wishes,
For health and happiness to all.

The world need not be the third act
        of Earthly Delights;
I persist to maintain a light and pleasant eye,
One as such that sees all flowers as beautiful
        without compare...
And the magnificent Gum as a teacher,
        sustained by all elements—
Great phoenix of the land, abundant in reality,
Not a bird, but a tree;
To die, and be reborn, in fire—
True magic spun in cycles.

This heat; this energy;
This intoxicating, welcome insomnia.
How gladly we continue to thrive
        well after the summer sun sets,
Then rise in the early hours of the morning...
Too long in Winter we slept, rested;
In Spring, we woke and stretched
        our limbs and brought colour to our skin;

In this season of fire, we dance
        and swim and sing and fear not
        the anxieties of the dark…
How readily we embrace the Moon's glow,
Now admired by those whom rarely gaze
        towards the sky…
A second Sun; no longer does time feel
        in short supply.
I find myself gleefully reading 'til
        the young hours of the rising,
        enjoying the cool, comforting scent
        of nightly air mingle with the
        aroma of old books and freshly-washed
        linen…
Marvel at the simplicities of summer comforts.

I walk within a Monet vision.
A great impression of natural wonder;
So minimal…so harmless…
Yet so rich;
Colour, an unspoken currency of the soul
That even night could not rob,
For it, too, beholds a navy palette,
        accents of purple and green

        and a generous dusting of stars.
Even on a New Moon, the world is
        never truly dark…
Instead, reveals other-worldly phosphorescence—
Hypnotised, I welcome another realm of life.
        Ancient. Unending…

Taken for granted, this life of mine.
Summer patterns open my Eye;
I lay upon the earth and hope
        to dissolve the worst parts of myself…
To cast out darkness, blindness,
A build within my fleshy shell
        something new:
Balanced.
Harmonious.
Synchronised.

As I write, I am exposed to my own
        hypocrisies,
Like a true temperament exposed by heat.

Crack through this false god-like structure,
Our feeble, pious charade…

And worship the ground we walk on.

Of course, when there are summers,
There are storms.
        O, storm, rich in rain,
Bathe us in noise,
In nitrogen flashes of light:
Feed us...
Sing us to sleep with the
        lullaby of the season;
        Raindrops on rooftops...
A palpable wave of weather,
A wrestle between winds
Whipping through the wispy peak
        of the young, flexible She-Oak;
To come together, collide
        with the clash of a heavenly cymbal—
A cry, not of anger, but of
        exalted ecstasy.
May we brave the electric light
And meet the wet ground with bare feet
        and open mouths, to receive pure
        medicine on our tongues.
Let me drink, as does the grass...

As does the bird and the ant...
As does the flower and the field...
I fill my cup, and with thanks,
> drink the last drop.

Again, such exhilarating insomnia!
Only on balmy nights do I chase away
> ideas of sleep
In favour of putting pen to paper,
> and spill my mind in ink upon the page.
Contemplations pour as golden sap
> tapped from the ready maple tree
> during such fine nights;
Words tangle as grape vines, ready
> to be plucked and pressed and made into
> the finest wine.
Although I do not partake in the drink,
Such excitement of play of vocabulary
> renders me wide-eyed and rambling—
I imagine I scarcely make sense!
Except, perhaps, to those who share minds
> colourful and entangled
> like mine;
Drunk on the magic and possibilities of words.

A great photosynthesis happens within us;
Energy made and energy shared...
Green-red blooded.
I can still hear the laughter of
        my neighbours well into the night,
And their laughter brings me happiness.

The days around Litha bring such wonderment and adventure:
Gathering seekers of thrills—hiking, theme parks, horror movies;
Such bravery we muster, such strength,
As if the closer sun has hardened our nerves and
        burned away our fears...
I, too, place my nerves to the side
        and face the scares head-on.

I turn my back on a million eyes;
I do not wish to receive their gaze.
I wish only to be seen by the Sun,
        The Stars,
        The Moon,
        The birds,
        and all the creatures that live in simplicity.

In this race of Life, believed to be run
        against Time,
I run in the opposite direction,
And find Time more infinitely.

I call the day *my home*;
I do not wish for strangers,
        For toxicity of the spirit,
        For hatred and pests
To enter my home, unwelcome,
And so, too, shall remain my day.

How remarkable of an illusion is reality!
It is but a mirage in the middle of the road—
And we can see then what is usually unseen;
Heat breaking in waves through air.

We are colour—
A collection of prisms of light;
To look upon a photo in black and white
        and know what colours lie beneath,
It must be a power within us,
Within our eyes…
Within our minds…

Within our souls...
To look beyond the surface
        and see colour,
        beauty,
        life,
And something else entirely.

Everything around Her is Perfect;
Those hazy summer nights with air full of smoke from a bushfire—
        A new generation of plants will be born;
Those earthquakes that rattle us—
        The birth of new mountains and new ecosystems;
That flood or that tsunami—
        Cleans rivers and moves seeds to thrive in new locations;
I know it may not look that way,
But imagine you are the seed,
Waiting for the necessary extremities
In order to grow.

The magic in my life flows beneath me,
In worlds beneath the dirt

       that thrive and speak
       all the languages of the earth;
That magic, that healing, when unaltered,
Seeps into the abundant harvest;
       A message from Earth to tell us what
       we truly need.
I take the food of the seasons,
       their flavours and their favours,
       and imbue them with
       my very own magic.
In my kitchen, I cook for you.
I wish you all the best,
And that my food gives you strength,
In life,
In health,
In happiness.

What are you waiting for?
The Sun shines its face for you
       every day.
Look up and embrace its smiles
For they give you light
and show up to Life,
       just as the Sun shows up for you.

How tightly it holds onto you—
A hand to hold you through the dark,
A hand to guide your path
       so you may witness every step
       and see the trail behind you...
And ahead of you.
Even in the night,
       In the pitch-black moments of your life,
The Sun is always there,
       Beside you,
       Constantly...

On the ground, I still lay,
A hollow frame waiting to be filled.
Vines erupt from the earth and embed
       themselves into my veins;
A nature injection, replenish depleted stores...
Make my green eyes even brighter
       To see the vibrations 'round all living
       things.

I wish to slow down,
To see flowers wilt
and leaves change colour...

To watch the bread dough rise
        and the steady sun set…
To see the seeds sprout shoots and
        signal their arrival to the sun…
To feel heartbreak and happiness, completely…
To watch handmade projects take fruit…
To watch the grass grow, the paint dry,
        the time go by,
Intentionally.

In this time, we feel invincible.
Taking advantage of the gift of daylight,
To learn new skills and hone our craft;
To visit friends and loved ones;
Because never more, than this time
Have we felt more alive—
Like the pop of fireworks
Or the rush of a waterfall;
We ignite and announce our earthly presence…

Only if we acknowledge that:

One day, the street lights will go out,
Our phones die, TV unplugged, fridge warm;

Then, we will have to turn back to Her,
To reconnect with Her roots and Her fruits.
I just pray that when that occurs,
She has not turned her back on us…

How perfect it is
That the wind blows harder
When the flowers and the trees
Need to scatter their seeds.

Lie on the ground, feel secure
On the steady soil.
Feel your growing space merge
      with the growing grass,
Your breath in sync with the wind
      as it softly slides between nostrils
      and swirls in sounds inside your skull.

There must be balance in all things;
Magnetic partners—attraction and repulsion…
The world needs the strong and the loud,
But it also needs the soft and the quiet.
      This does not mean they're weak:
The speaker needs a listener…

The wounded fighter needs a healer...
Not all the world can be action and noise,
We would drown and burn
        and commit atrocities for the sake of
        silence;
A selfish silence, only to hear one's self speak...
Be kind to the keepers of the quiet;
The gentle souls who tend and treat
and hold peace within a teacup...
        a piece of paper...
        a flower bed...
        an open window...
        clean sheets softly flapping in the sunshine.

A dark thought tumbles around my mind;
        My mind, made of flint
        And the thought, a stone—
What if I don't wake up tomorrow?
Stone and flint collide
        and create a spark;
        a curious contemplation...
A glimpse into the fickleness of Time
        as it ticks away with its hands—
Its hands! Its face!

We have tried to humanise Time...
Time is a seed, a snowflake,
A single, falling leaf,
A ray of sunlight...
There is Time, and there is *my* time.
Tomorrow, my time may end;
Or tomorrow, I wake to find all Time has gone.
What would this mean?
Every morning, I shall open my eyes
And whisper to the Now;
'Thank you.'

Multitudinous Incarnadine

A dusk in sanguine, I shall never forget:
Those crimson castles of the sky
And golden paths of welkin way;
My eyes raise to lilac airs between curtains blue,
Drawn apart and dipped in tangerine.
A sensual glide of colour.

Earth's lover is close tonight,
All aglow and blushing; embarrassment
Also reflected in my rosy cheeks.
(Can she see? Me? As I, her?)
O, rutilant Moon, I feel Earth sigh,
Pull you nearer, as you with her.
Ombré waves move as hands to touch.

Salty summer breeze slides over my skin,
Shaking me with the indescribable sense
Of seeing two Goddesses meet.
Heat stings under flesh at the sight
Of a passion that is not my own,
Yet shines in all of space and where eyes see.
Earth sheds shame and inhibition like a robe.

Fingers of light stretch from each cosmic body,
Lambent; garnet streams slither 'round Earth's throat
As the Moon draws to her side,
And in the last fragments of the Sun's descent,
All is bathed in the spark of their embrace.
The night, for a moment, pushed aside;
Through my window, multitudinous incarnadine.

Mångata

Waning; weaving; whole; Mirrored Goddess glow...
She pulls with ease on currents,
Aquatic robes of liquid silk around Earth's frame.
Unity;
Beyond the corruption of Man,
It reflects upon Ocean's face;
The child of Their consummation
        that swells and protests with Their power,
Pulling apart ships that seek to destroy.
A universal union,
No Gods could tear apart,
Hypnotised by delicate lights on crimson seas,
Mångata; fingers clasped together in celestial communion,
Older than Time itself.

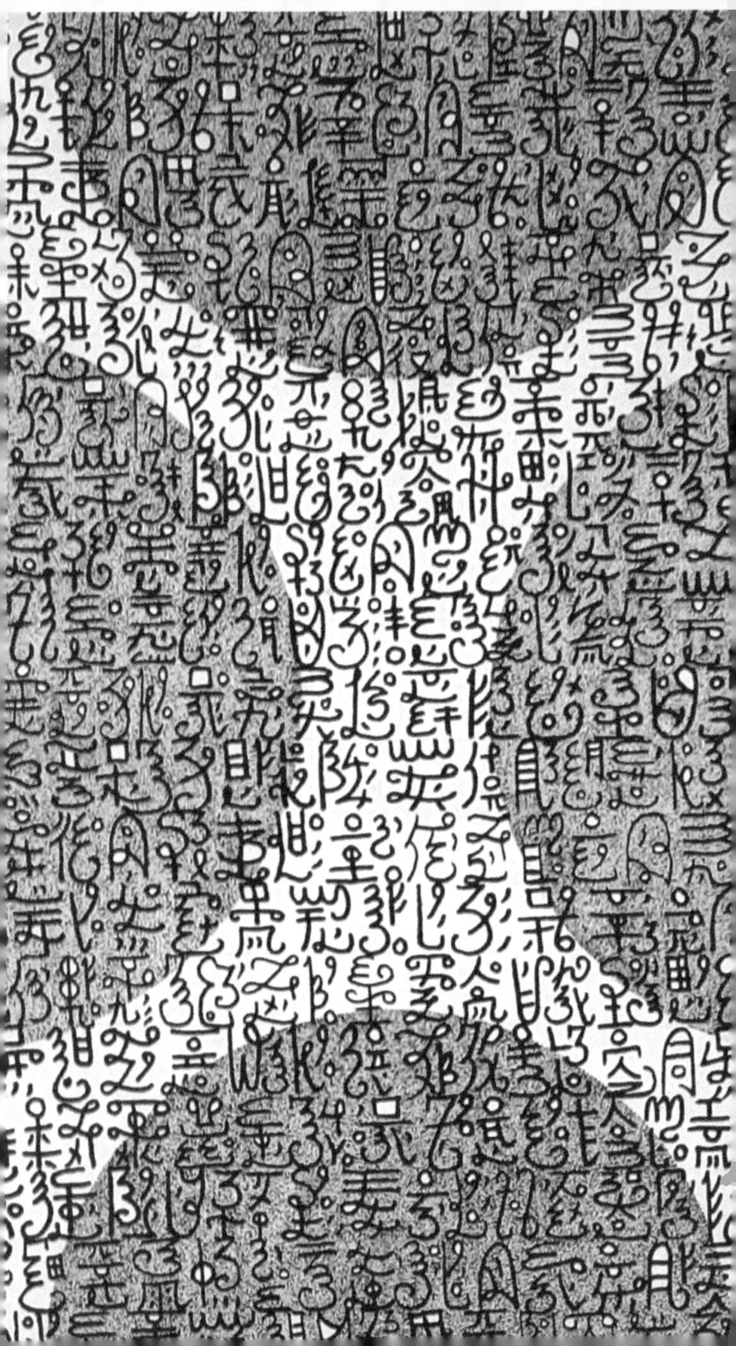

The Prayer

The morning begins in pale clementine,
        and the evening in rich grapefruit;
The day (and night) encased
In orange parentheses.
If I imagine the World a bowl of fruit,
Life begins to taste a little sweeter.
Dionysus, was this your intention?
To get high on fruit and wine
        and dine on simple pleasures:
The mouth feels as much of the world as the hands do.
Dionysus, does the world taste sound like I do?
Does real, unbridled laughter feel warm and heavy in their mouths, too?
Did we all, once, taste cries like salt water
        as they poured in anguish out of our
        throats?
Dionysus, does the world smell sights like I do?
Warm sunlight smells like bread and lemons and old books.
        I like that.
Dionysus, would you be angry if I spoke to Apollo
for a moment?

For it is the Sun that gives me greater pleasure.
Apollo, I heard that the Sun will swallow the Earth.
Is this true?
Will the Sun know Saturn's grief?
Or are we but an apple in space,
        His fingers ever closer to grasping us in the
        darkness?
Perhaps, Apollo, we are all just part
        of one celestial fruit bowl,
Relishing in our own sweetness
And bathing in the warm release of
        the Sun's citric juices.
The morning begins in tangerine,
        and the evening in blood orange;
The night (and day) encased
In orange parentheses,
Falling away like peel.

Ocean Blue

The beach is hours away;
Yet I still smell the salty waves
And the sweet scent of sunlight on sand.
Driving 'round sharp bends in mountainous,
country bushland,
I imagine every turn will bring me
To gaze upon the ocean.
It's like magic;
To mistake the blood in your ears for
        the rushing tides,
And to feel breezes upon skin carrying the
        distant spray of salt water.
I am not fond of the colour blue,
But in such moments, I crave it—
The way blue moves…the way blue sounds…
The way blue pulls us in with a gravitational
        promise of serenity.
The beach is hours away;
And for the first time,
I miss the colour blue,
        Which is strange,
        Because the sky is blue, too.

Student of Life

> *'Ainsi tout passe sur la terre*
> *Esprit, Beauté, Grâce, Talent*
> *Telle est une fleur éphémère*
> *Que renverse le moindre vent.'*
> *Unknown*

I know nothing.
If you were to accumulate all the knowledge
of the world,
I, myself, know nothing.

I am okay with that.

I ask a lot of questions.
If I were to collect every one of my questions,
A great many volumes of books containing my curiosity
        would line my bookshelves.
Many I will never know the answers to;
And that is okay.

I will never know why the sky is *blue*,
The secrets of the Voynich manuscript,

Or the lost contents of the Library of Alexandria.
Perhaps some things are too great to be known;
Is there really some kind of God, and
Could our fragile human minds handle true divinity?
Is faith the blanket, the soft, dampening, safe place in our minds
That allows us to process all we feel but cannot explain?
Clouds act as the padded walls 'round this earthly room,
        to keep us safe.

I know nothing about the divine,
The invisible hand that guides us mere mortals
        along our destined paths.
I only know what I feel;
        (Even though I don't know what I feel),
And the inner beliefs, the personal truths
That create my own identity.

What would happen if the Earth started spinning in the opposite direction?

I watch, from the safety of my house,

All those creatures unbothered by the rain.
The spider still sits in her web,
Protected only by the few strands she has gathered
    to create her gossamer barrier.
Those tiny birds, barely bigger than
    the fat droplets that fall upon them,
    cold bullets from the sky—
They shake them off and continue their feast
    on the grevillea.
The horse in its vast grass kingdom
    doesn't move.
I wonder if it feels the rain at all?
Yet here I sit, in the dry and warm,
Wondering when the human stamina
For all of Earth's seasons
Began to fade.

Just how much history is yet to be uncovered?
Should we leave it in its resting place?
Howard Carter, glorified grave robber,
    found the tomb of Tutankhamun.
How marvellously backwards it is, what we can learn
from the dead!
The life of a person etched into the hidden crevasses

of bone.
To what god do archaeologists worship?
Mr Carter, how does the north wind feel against your spirit?
You have your own grave to plunder now.

How much must be destroyed in this pursuit of knowledge?

My belief that the Earth breathes
And feels our presence,
Is one often scorned.
I see trees dance, and birds in conversation;
      All is perfect.
Every blade of grass is a hair,
      a stitch, a thread
           that helps hold the world together.
I observe when each flower opens their heart,
      and learn from them the meaning of softness.
When it is my time to join the grass
And the fallen leaves,
I pray my spirit taken away,
Curled within the petals of a lotus.

What I do know is this:
An insatiable thirst for learning.
To know languages and science,
Horticulture, history, religion.
Come, people of the world,
Let me be!
I want to know how much knowledge
        one human brain can hold.
To explore the lands of sleep
And become a cartographer of dreams.

To feel and to know walk hand in hand
Along the longitudinal fissure;
The canyon of my brain,
To remind me that not all the world's answers
Can be found in books.
There are experiences that must be touched:
Remember, remember, every cell in my body,
remember,
The weave of the papyrus,
The smooth scales of a snake,
The body of a Bodhi tree,
Mountain mist sitting on your skin,
The warmth of the Sun that travelled space to find you.

Memento mori.

I often ponder: 'Were I God, what would I do?'
This is my hardest question,
With no answer out there in the world for me to find.
All those beings.
How does the Earth withstand our feet?
Our cars, trains, cranes and drills.

Forgive me, for a moment, if you will,
As I endeavour to see life through
The eyes of a god...here on Earth,
The good and the evil...to know it all,
Indifferently.

I stretch my arms into the darkness,
Embrace, and search for heartbeats—
Exiled star with its last ember of light;
I crush your diamond body...pressure, building heat,
Scatter you as far as you dare venture.
There is no end to your sight, for I have made you infinite.

The spaces between light dance with colours;

What I see is beautiful…and the darkness,
Yet to be painted, is beautiful, too.

A star dies, a star reborn…
Rainbow nebulas, black holes;
Planets swirl in sacred geometry…
Bodies gathered around a celestial campfire,
        spinning around its flames
        at their own unique pace.

Beyond this, I can scarcely imagine.
Beyond this, I know not.
Perhaps divinity is what we create
        with what we have
        and what we feel
        in the present moment.
I create. I write. It is divine.
What I create comes into being—
        unlock my inner goddess.

But bless me with omnipresence,
So, I my look upon every inch
Of this vast blue planet
And observe…

Sweet Lorelei, what songs do you sing?
Are they songs of sadness and sorrow,
Words faded behind the alluring symphony
      of your voice?
Upon the cliffs, the wind carries your song
      through rocks and across waves
      that crash at your feet.
They, too, jump towards your
Hypnotic sound.

Why, of all smiles, is the Mona Lisa's
      so well protected?
What secrets hide behind those lips?
Is it you, dear painter, who hides himself
      behind those eyes?
Your work, your soul, never finished,
Has the world wrapped in fascination.

To see the caverns of crystals,
The quartz bloodline of the planet.
I bet it sings underground;
      Millions of fragments humming low,
      Gemstone monks in sacred space,
Veil the fragile veins from

The destruction above.

To be omnipotent—
        now, that I do not want.
To never be amazed by new discoveries;
Not to the world, but to me.
Take me to Hermopolis
        or to the black obelisk of Nectanebo,
            the door taken from its home.
Teach me astrology and medicine,
Mathematics and astronomy.
But Thoth, please tell me this,
If past lives may be true:
        Was my heart feather-light?

Where do we go, when the body no longer breathes?
Souls passed, merge, combine memory and spirit,
Roam the world together in search of a heart
Large enough to let them all in.

I wish to see the bottom of the deepest ocean,
With a clarity as though I bring with me
        a ray of sun.
Ancient creatures of the dark,

      we are foreign to each other.
I will not touch, but leave you in peace,
For now, I know you're there;
I'm sure your purpose in this vast ecosystem
Is greatly unappreciated,
      if understood at all.

Who was the first to place honey on a wound?
Who was the first to heat metal for swords?
What was the world's first word?

I have heard it said
That to predict the future,
One must study the past.
There was no past with this many souls.
No past so collapsed under its own humanity.
But I have faith in those who try:
Those who continue the knowledge and skill
      of our ancestors.
In the future, we will turn to them,
Those who preserve the past,

      Keeping the traditions worth knowing
      Alive.
What is to be gained from withholding knowledge?
I suppose that is a question for those who write our histories.
Oh, how I wish to roam freely through the vaults
      of the Vatican Archives.

To seek treasure; to solve the unknown;
The lost tributes of Napoleon...
The cryptogram of La Buse...
The lost eggs of Fabergé...
The Ark of the Covenant...
The Three Brothers...
Jack the Ripper...
The lost colony of Roanoke...
Is this to be our vice?
An adrenaline-fuelled race
      To find what is lost,
      To know what is unknown,
In the miniscule amount of time
Our hearts still beat.
Mystery, it appears,
Is a core ingredient of Life.
We are fuelled by food, water, oxygen,

and curiosity.

The world has its secrets;
Many have died to find them...
Many have died to keep them...

Teach me how to recognise the giant hogweed
        from the Lace of Queen Anne;
To steer clear of the visions of the Belladonna;
To see through the deceitful charms of an Angels' Trumpet;
And to not accept food or shelter from the
Manchineel Tree.

I do not wish to die due to my own intellectual
failings.

The darkest corner of technology
        deciphered the devil's letter of Sister Maria.
Trust and faith may be tested here.
This system works for no one.

What were the lives of those
        who hold up the streets of Paris,
Those who guard the *Barrière d'Enfer*;

A foundation of bones *intra muros*,
With no shortage of warnings:
Arrête! C'est ici l'empire de la Mort.
Beliefs and superstitions, come forth!
Does the soul linger after death?
Do the human remains from the past frighten you?
Come and see,
        I am sure they mean no harm.

What is the best way to respect the dead?

To become art after death,
To make beauty from the macabre—
Great chapels made of bones;
Cherubs cling from skulls in one…
Another overseen with silent prayers from exhumed friars.
To know Life is to acknowledge Death.

I do not fear the unknown,
I only wish to study it.
As I age,
        Things unknown will become known,
        And things known will become unknown.
We write, because we cannot extract memories,

        knowledge, dreams, ideas,
        from a body that has met its mortal end.
Our thoughts do not imprint themselves in words
        on the inside of our skulls,
        or within the tissue of my brain.
To write; to learn; to preserve;
No matter the accuracy,
May be one of humanity's greatest
accomplishments.
To pursue knowledge has become its own
        form of art.

Fragrance

There is a scent that lingers on season's shoulders,
Permeates beneath the cloudless blue.
Trees breathe, pores opening,
Exhale;
Hints of Earth, of sunscreen, of fresh air,
And a nameless perfume on tongue tips.
Bathing in sunlight, a comfortable warmth.
I ask others, 'Do you smell it, too?
Mouth-watering, intoxicating,
Nature's pleasant fragrance?'

No one has.

It has become my secret delight;
A moment shared in shade, on air,
Whispers passed on winds that fill lungs—
A scent that calms; for with it,
As it tosses hair and tantalises the senses,
The promise of a good day,
For such a scent, with no earthly name
Is never there on a rainy day.

Horizon

The rain is delicious;
An incredible sweetness of taste,
And an ineffable scent—
Descending upon us,
It can only be described as heavenly,
For that must be its place of origin...
That fine line
Where the ocean meets the sky
And the two plains merge—
The Sun calls out heaven's name
With its chorus of rays
As it passes by:
Horizon!

Shelter

Does the hollow tree still breathe?
The one in whose trunk I rest
        to wait for the storm to pass.
Do I nestle within its ribs or its embrace?
I am not the first to use this wooden sanctuary;
Gentle carvings and declarations of love
        line the inner walls.
There is an incredible feeling of safety,
To sit inside such a large tree.
It barely moves in the storm,
        makes almost no sound.
Great guardian, I imagine your roots
        grow immeasurably deep.

Midnight Sun

The summer midnight has a glow,
Grey and mysterious;
Time does not linger in the shade of the sky—
Deceptively hiding the Sun, though its
       ascent hours away...
How peculiar, that in the depths of night,
It does not seem all that dark.

Summerland

Caelitis. Supernal. Temenos.

This fractal realm that shimmers,
The landscapes casting rainbow swirls
      as though cleansed by celestial light.
The body, though it appears to have form,
Vibrates in every cell, multiplying slowly,
      to fall between your fingers
      like sand and stardust.
This is your home now,
      for the time being.
Bathe in the sunlight and drink in its rays.
Watch your rainbow skin shine brighter,
      millions of vibrant grains of life.
Walk amongst the singing grass
      and eat the jewelled fruit.
Be whole again, in spirit.
Do not fear the fall;
You'll land as soft and scattered as rain,
To live on and on.

Murr-ma

I finally find myself at the beach,
Standing where the water meets the sand,
Engaged in a murr-ma ritual.
A little girl and her even younger brother
       fearlessly throw handfuls of wet sand at
       each other,
Toss themselves into the oncoming waves.
In my years, I know as they don't,
       how rough and unforgiving the ocean can be;
But today, the ocean is gentle and playful,
As though careful not to disturb the laughter of children—
       playing in nature and enjoying its gifts;
They collect shells and build sandcastles...
The boy covers his sister in seaweed
       and claims he's caught a mermaid...
They search rock pools for crabs and creatures
       that suck on their fingers...
The girl finds beauty in a washed-up abalone shell,
       with its pearlescent sheen...
They rescue jellyfish...
They spy an octopus with blue rings...
They talk to whales through holes in stones...

They collect spume and blow it into bubbles...
They feel as though nothing in the world
        could hurt them as they lay back and bob
        like boats over the waves,
The sun warm on their faces and sand caressing their skin
Like the gentle hand of a mother.

The Snake and the Spider

As the setting summer sun
Sunk beneath the singing trees,
A snake of substantial size
Searched for his evening meal.
He sought and scoured
Through shrubs and trees,
Behind rocks, in holes and
Underneath flowers.
He searched high and low,
As stars started to shine,
But the slow and starving snake
Soon found trouble of another kind.

A web unlike any other,
Woven wide between the woodland trees,
Ensnared the startled snake,
Wrapped tighter, he wrestled the weave.
For the owner of the web,
She too was weak and hungry,
And woven all week the white, wide, web,
To catch all who came wandering.
Woken by the wriggling web,

She walked upon the weave,
And the snake was shocked to see the spider
As substantially large as he.

'I wove all week, without a tweak,
Now I will have food to eat!'

'Silly spider, can't you see,
I will slide out of this weave.'

'My web is strong, I wove it so,
To catch all creatures down below.
Wriggle more and you will know
How much tighter it will go.'

The starving snake stopped his struggle,
Instead, would use his smarts.
He needed to save all his strength
To escape the spider's grasp.

'Spider, I see you have made a mistake,
To wrap me in weave, how long would it take?
My size and my stamina, how long do you feel
It would take for me to be the perfect meal?

I see you do not feast on flesh
Until it's rotten and soft.
For such a starving spider,
How much longer have you got?'

'I'll wait, and wait, and wait,
And watch as you grow weak,
Watch as you waste away,
I can wait an extra week.'

'You seem sure you could survive,
Yet your hunger saps your strength.
You shall perish before my time is done,
And I shall be the stronger one.'

'Perhaps you would forget, snake,
That your appetite has not been whet.
And you were weak enough to wander
Into my waiting woven web.
We shall wait to see who is stronger,
The hunter or the prey?
And with time we shall know who
Will live to see another day.'

And so, they waited, the foolish pair,
To see whose strength would win,
To see who would give in
And declare the other victory fair.
Yet in their stubborn resolute,
The third day saw both dead;
The snake and the spider,
And the great, white, wide web.

Ocean Beds

Ocean beds, I find myself dreaming there;
A blanket of blue, bubbles, seaweed and
Fluid, dancing ribbons of rainbow light.
The cool current caresses my shoulders,
And I imagine myself a creature
Adrift in weightless motion beneath waves.
Turquoise waters shimmer bright light upon
White sands like crystalised sugar, salt
And the sweet sensations of summer heat,
That dries and kisses my skin with freckles.
Rhythmic waves slow down heartbeats, chasing calm
And unearthing buried laughter within.
Those tantalising coils of light wrap
Around my ankle and tempt me to float,
Above ocean beds, and just simply dream.

Leap Year

February 29th, where have you been hiding?
I seek something lost
        and I need you to guide me.
For four years you have charged your energies
        and drank the Sun in secret.
Has its liquid fire filled your cup?
Or were you engaged in celestial consummation?
I planted seeds of myself
        long ago,
        to see what fruit they'd bear.
But I lost myself along the way,
Pieces buried, I know not where.

Leap year, on this rare February day,
Guide me to the shoots of my soul,
So I may make a garden of myself,
And feel a little more whole.

The Song of Mabon

'Tis the season to celebrate decay;
A romanticism of the fleetingness of Life.
O, Glory to Death!
We acknowledge and salute you
As you pass through with your parade
Of fallen leaves and fog-hugged mornings.

If Spring celebrates the face of Earth,
Then Autumn is its spirit.
More connected to the ground, we become;
Cinnamon, nutmeg, clove,
Spices of wood
Paired with the abundant harvest
That grows within the dirt.

Shuffle through sepia-stained memories;
Polaroids of the past.
The scrapbook of sunnier days.
It's time to slow down and reflect...
Sleep is coming soon.

Nostalgia-fuelled dreams,

It is there I wish to stay.
To watch, again, my inner seed grow,
Change,
Wither and bloom;
Remind myself that I am not yet
        in the Autumn of my life,
But it cannot be Summer forever.

The ground is cloaked in auburn patchwork,
Draped over us, holding warmth to the earth.
The burnt soldiers of summer can rest now.
Return to the land you so bravely defended.

Those leaves like small fires fall without fear.
Piles of their harmless embers
Now a hearth for tired creatures.
Gather the dying flames, but do not extinguish—
The residents of the dirt need a blanket, too.

Sunlight is more precious than gold.
The time to drink its elixir dwindles
        with each passing day.
Drink what you can and be merry.

The world weaves together wonder and woe
To stitch the tattered shroud
That split, just for a moment,
To let souls sail by, silent as the grave.

Mabon, you make the months of your presence
        as bright as the spring,
When there are no clouds to block the sun
And every ray imbues shades of warmth
Upon all it touches.
How selfless is he, the Sun!
Doing all he can to keep comfort in our souls
As we approach the colder season.
Gourds become bundles of sunlight
Scattered across the ground.

Plant your bulbs and your prayers.
The earth will keep them safe
And all shall be answered in Spring.
Practice patience and all shall come to pass.

The Rolling Fields of Sorghum

Bronze soldiers stand to attention in the summer sun,
Peeling back the green of their youth.
Copper as far as the eye can see,
        sways in synchronicity.
Autumn draws ever near,
And the soldiers celebrate their win
        in the fight against the fire;
The rolling hills scattered in their
        bronze-coloured armour.
Ribbons of light bless their heads
        in ripples like gentle river-beds
        kissed by soft winds.
Before their passing, during the final
        rains of the season,
They stand as one, brothers-in-arms,
Their final crusade;
To hold the rolling fields
Together.

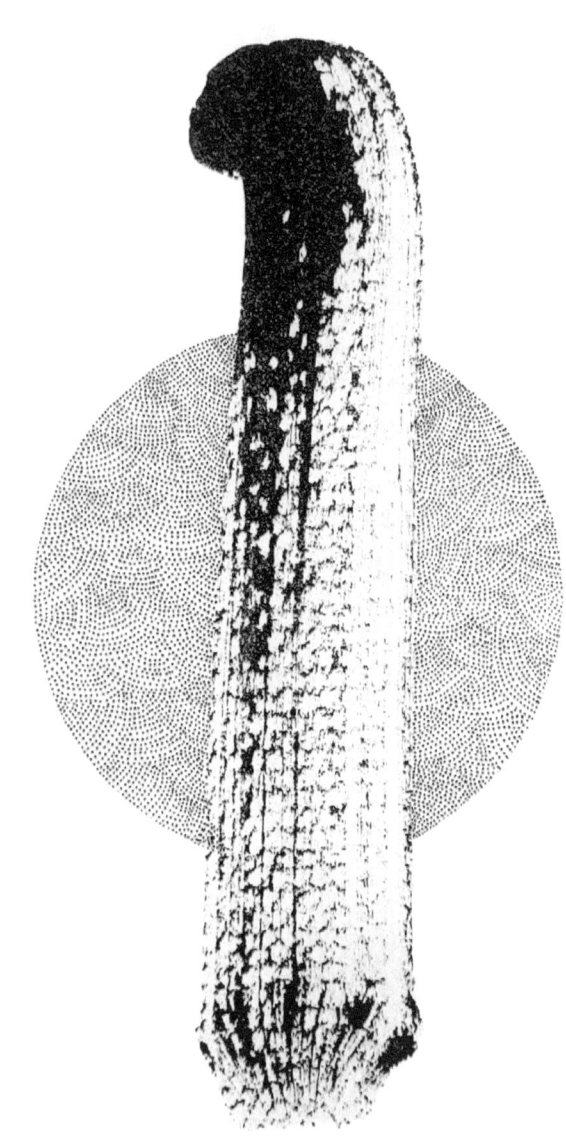

Virago

We still love roses, despite their thorns;
The oleander, despite its poison and itch.
These are not flaws, but suits of armour.

Do not remove me of my armour;
Though my words may cut and sting.
Do not cut down my spine
Because I dared to stand up for myself.
Do not blind me because I dared
        to face my fears, my enemies.

I am Judith, with my sword
        hidden under my bed;
Rust and dull removed,
It now waits, sharpened.

Alyssum

A single flower plucked and consumed
        and my anger did die:
Such an emotion—blood boils in inner basements below
        and the machines made of muscle
        squeeze out scalding steam;
Engine coals in the pit sit hot and heavy
And the vessel is ready to ignite
        and unleash its full power,
        showcasing potential madness.
Were I to eat the whole branch,
Would I become sane, or sombre?

A ribcage full of roses

A ribcage full of roses stings,
Yet sweetly smells of sadness.

Blood-red, pomegranate drips,
And earthly buds do bloom.
A single one I do pick
With amaranthine fingertips,
And place the bud between my lips;

I set the bud alight.

Ashes flitter, butterflies,
Smoke of mauve and blue.
With green-shot eyes, I step inside
A diamond, wooded labyrinthine,
The entrance, this world, upside-down;

The roses fall away.

Houred moments, clock hands—four,
Both forward, back, they roam,
And dreams go swiftly floating by,

Up to a ribboned, orchid sky,
With a sigh, I close my eyes;

And wake up to the day.

Verve

Restlessly, my brain does speak in tidal ebb,
Shrouded, foggy, cyan peaks collide within my head,
Boldly breaking hands of Time; a tongue of Language bruised,
And seeks around the mouth to find a word that's rarely used.
A concerto of letters glissando 'round my teeth, bloom in the bass of my throat,
And yet they catch before I speak…
For the verve demands a coloured coat,
And an image we can carry home in the pocket of our skull;
The inner recesses of the bone where all the world can feel so dull
Until we adorn it with paint, in colours never heard, and those of hues yet to be described by any earthly word.
Such wonderment, that I can paint with my voice, purely with the choice of my words and my dedication spent
To every stroke and curve, and thus, begin to build the verve;

Rolling brio rumbles from my diaphragm as thunder, and 'round the room, here and now, I tear the eldritch clouds asunder,

From this spot, begins to grow, an image now that I do sew

Stitch by stitch, line by line, into this internal world of mine;

This world of mine, I now present, for your baffled entertainment.

Because passing through this open space, from my lips to your brain,

I can paint a picture of pain; raw, red fingertips and the slow stabbing pace of pulse that tweaks on muscle strings like a marionette.

Or perhaps a picture of sadness—the colour: cold; one you won't forget, as a hand around your throat takes hold.

But how does one paint joy?

Do I paint mine, or yours?

For I see, in the space between shoulder-blades, the body stores its own album of colour and peace, and it radiates through the blood with heat;

Seeded roots begin to grow and wrap their many tendrils 'round bone.

From this place grows a garden bed, down your
spine and 'round your head, 'til spores
release through waves of laughter, melt into the
pores of another, thereafter building a garden of
their own.
Yet, all these acrylic and watercolour words fail, if
your imagination pales their vibrancy and reduces
them to a string of sounds and curves, and thus,
disregard the fragile verve.

The Dancer – 2

A man, barefoot and shirtless
Dances down a crowded street,
His face smiling towards the sun
In a sea of bent and broken necks.
Those who look up, judge,
And immediately assume his actions
      are the result of needles or pills,
      of alcohol or insanity.
He is labelled an addict; a hippie; a nutcase;
But he knows—he knows how to be happy.
Your resentment is just a mirror held
      up to your jealousy;
How is someone that happy? Feel so free?
Could that be me?
I see the stares of passers-by,
Their judgement and their hate.
One person steps forward to stop the man from dancing—
But he is not hurting anyone!
      Nor obstructing them...
I pick myself up and join him in dance;
Two souls choosing to be happy,

And finding a natural high in the
        surrender of our human Egos—
Energy, free-flowing as the wind...
Here and Now.

Lungs

Deep down; death beds await,
The last homely breath is held,
And in the boil of poison and bait,
A carcass cavern; coral and bone,
Sheds away from someone's home, and
Exposes them to our own glorified filth.
Beneath the salt and spume, a world groomed
For glass tanks and dinner tables, and ploughed
From the roots; torn and tumbled,
To adorn someone's fireplace mantle.
These lungs, a delicate serving squeezed
And shaved and hung,
And wrung of their breath, a face of choking
White, gasping beneath the blue,
'Til once upon a future night,
We start gasping, too.

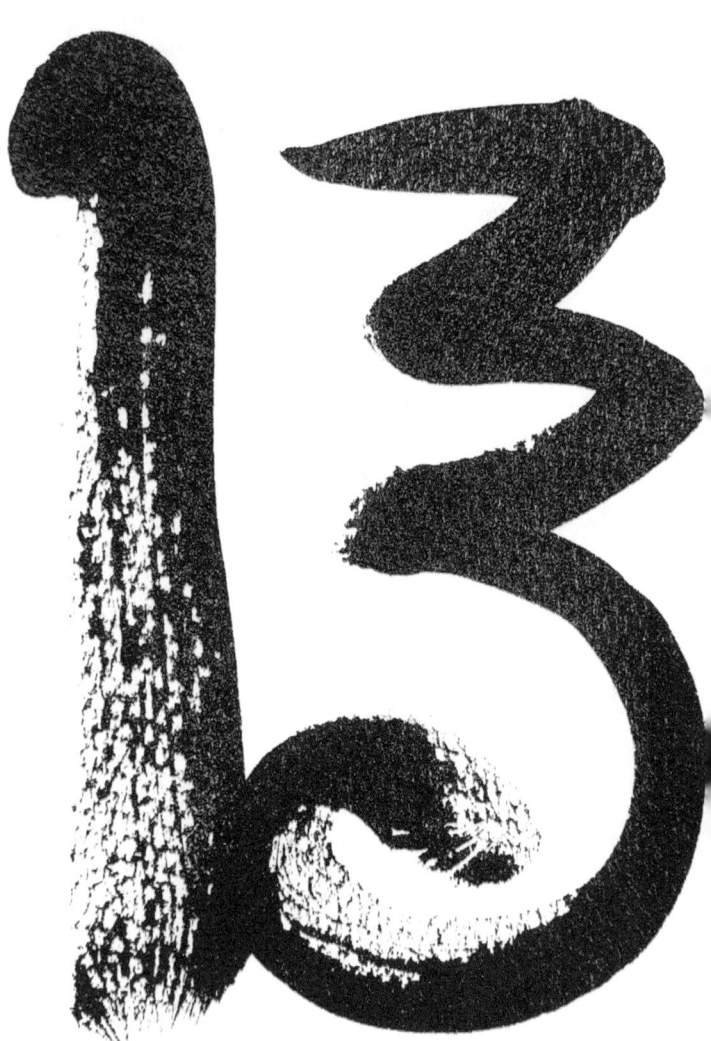

Hawk

Grace has fallen.
It lies as a single wing, wind-waving
        on the dividing line of the road...
Icarus of the sky, flew too close to the ground,
Into the path of smoking chariots
        held together with glue-like-death.
Master predator taken down by a hollow bullet;
Feathers spread as a hand full of knives,
        bound to lose from the beginning
        against the metal lion.

Dies Irae

Not from heaven shall Wrath descend,
But from Her womb, rise to meet us all,
For she grows weary of her love and pretend
Not to shiver with broken, aching appal.

Left in the Garden of Earthly Delights,
When the ground sinks beneath the burning dark,
Returning to a grim grisaille
With no chance of another divine spark.

Purple Hyacinths

And had he come with the dying flowers
Upon gravestones and tabletops alike,
Still, none would have seen him. A ghost anew,
But with a fleshy envelope, he walks
As a messenger of his solitude.
Ever fair, he moves like wind through columns.
His breath carries no sound, nor a whisper,
For only trees can understand the breeze;
And he lives in a barren wasteland
Of endless noise filled with constant chatter
As shallow as puddles in lands of drought.

He moves with all the silence of shadows;
This solitary spirit. But I see,
For he wears a coat of humble hue and
Seeks not the false treasures of modernity.
Had he more a voice to speak, he wouldn't.
Coffin nails, words wielded as weapons
Will lay the final blow on wounded souls,
And no longer is the pen mightier
Than the sword, as razor words seek to kill.
He drifts by an adolescent headstone

Adorned with purple hyacinths—ponders,
What end requires such an apology?
Delivered too late. Live with your regret.

He wanders on; by rivers and down streets,
Beneath shooting stars that search for faces,
The holy midnight ears are ringing and
Sirens call to full attention, to serve.
He watches as they pass him by, wild cries
From hastened chariots; these seraphim
Of the streets, deafened by their own noises.
He takes the hand of an innocent youth;
The Fates, it would seem, cut their string too short.
And he silently wept, as he knew now
The youth's life ended by one who made them.

Through broken dreams and endless screams, he walks,
Unseen, blind to those with mirrored visions.
Though he can talk, he chooses not; each word
Falls like stones in an ocean—the raging
Waves of narcissism deafen me. I
Cannot hear the call. So, he passes by,
Silently. While I tend to a field
Of purple hyacinths, in high demand.

The world moves in time of too late, as he
Moves in time with now, knowing the screams won't
Be heard until tomorrow. And when all
Graves are dressed with purple petals and tears,
We will look for him; the lonely spirit.

Gloaming

Reflections of a Summer's fading gold,
The trees all dressed in shimmering fires
That blanket the ground, not with flames,
But a smattering of dusk; the setting
Glow blends the fine line of the horizon,
As Earth mirrors Sky, and all at once the
World is hugged by Autumn's soothing embrace.

Whitman's sole

Tread carefully, gently, with a Whitman sole;
How much past rests within the dirt—
And future; long after I am gone...
Returned to earth, buried in-waiting
Beneath grass and leafy debris:
I am the grass!
        As are you...
Great green fields of souls—
Past, present, future:
The Fates made of stone and roots,
Our lifelines woven in mycelium.
Reflections of above, below...
A network of life!
Let us embrace and feed each other,
Talk through food and feeling—
O, such outstanding revelations!
Need not look toward the future and
        unanswered questions;
All lies beneath our feet,
Threads that bind life and death...
I see it start in the rapid spores
Feasting on a discarded apple core.

The Song of Yule

Winter, true winter,
I must admit, I have never experienced.
I have felt cold, I have felt grief,
I have seen the grey hold of the world
      and the trees stripped bare.
But blankets of white beyond sight—
      I can only imagine.
I have no doubt my imagination pales in comparison,
But it brings comfort to my mind's experience.

Winter reminds us of the power
      of breath;
      the privilege of full lungs.
Air, breath, once invisible
Now hovers in front of our faces;
Reminds us: breathe deep, breathe strong,
This foggy apparition proves you're still thriving.

Celebrate the darkness;
Slow down and rest, sleep.
Conserve yourself. The dance is coming,

All in divine timing.
Until then, breathe, sleep,
And move with peace.

If I should wake to a white winter,
A single step upon the snow—no,
I could not disturb such beauty!
I would sit on a step
And watch the sunlight dance
        across the fragile crystals,
Slowly melting throughout the day.

The cyclamen wakes from its warm slumber
And breathes in the cool, crisp air.
Teach me, mistress of the cold,
How to thrive when days are short
And the mornings are encased in ice.
I eagerly anticipate your guidance.

In Yule, we worship fire
And all the trees still dressed with green.
The world around us becomes so tactile;
Do not stay inside. Brave the cold
And brush your fingertips

    against the frost,
    the Oak needles,
    the plain garden stone—
Then revive them against
    the warm walls of
    a mug of tea.

The wheel has turned;
The Holly and the Oak duel.
The Oak shall win on this solstice day,
With the promise to reign in abundance
    as it signals the end of night
    and calls in the newborn Sun.

Do not abandon the Winter;
    do not run from its presence.
Winter has its equal purpose
Amongst the seasons.
For it to always be Spring or Summer
    would be to exhaust all our natural stores.
We appreciate warmer weather
When we have made it through the cold.

Do you not miss those nights?

As a child or an adult?
Those cold nights when your bed
        is laid with extra blankets;
Pulled right up to your chin,
You allow the blankets to cocoon you.
We are the winter bugs;
        warm and cozy,
            rubbing our feet together like crickets,
            trying to ignite an internal fire
            with friction.

Do not think the season so different from Summer.
When one clings onto the ice-cold handrail,
They are met with a burning sensation.

Give thanks to your
        house,
        bed,
        clothes,
        hot water,
        heater,
        blankets and fluffy socks;
Imagine winter without them.

See how the earth talks to you with fruit.
Winter is the season for citrus;
Oranges, lemons, grapefruits and mandarins
      grow for us in abundance.
She grows for us our medicine
      to keep us strong.
Perhaps all those warm and earthy colours
Do not belong to Fall, after all.
A small ball of juicy sunshine;
Consume readily and enjoy.

Coffee

Cars rush by chatty cafés,
Wheels squeal like sirens towards their destinations,
A great lane of hurry beside the slow
        hiss of steam and
        the stirring of silver spoons,
Bitter and blistered beans grind to a halt
        and ignite aromatic waves that linger
        invasively on the tongue;
Oxygen, roasted.
Two disjointed symphonies move
        between tables and meld together into
        melodies of mayhem and the mundane—
The music of the every man.

Everywhere

Stars reflected in the stillness of streams
        and the gentle trickle of time;
I can touch the heavens from here.
A bridge of flesh between worlds, I become,
And the universe swirls in gossamer pools
        around my hand; the other, skyward;
The sounds of space glissando over smooth stones.
Connected by source, spirit, and the
        symphonies of nature,
I find myself a being of multitudes,
In two places at once;
Both on the earth, and
Among the stars.

The Skimming Stone

A skimming stone hops with glee
Upon a frozen lake.
The sound had so enchanted me,
Another stone I did take.

A boring stone, not one remembered,
Nor one I would forget,
So plain and smooth and weathered
In the cold and frozen wet.

Nestled betwixt my fingers,
I turn it over thrice,
A moment in time lingers,
Then I cast it on the ice.

It slid with an echoed tune;
Euphoric, was what I heard,
The sound that came that winter's noon
Was the sound of a bird.

A simple stone, smooth and grey
From which the singing came;

Beside me, weathered pebbles lay,
Would their sound be the same?

And so, I threw the whole lot,
Entranced by what I heard...
For echoed back, the sound I got
Was a symphony of birds.

How brightly shine the stars of yonder!

How brightly shine the stars of yonder!
Yet shall we die with the same flaming brilliance?
Dreaming, beneath this eternal sky, I wonder
What awaits beyond its magnificence?
Are we not made the same as stars?
Do our eyes not hold their own constellations?
And when we die, do our dust and bones spread far
Enough to rest within their heavenly stations?
For we know, energy never dies, and our own must go on,
Back into the earth and skies, to the mortal realms
we came from.
So, if I shall not be a star, make me one with night,
To be the beast of darkness as I die amongst the
light.

I walked down the path of art

I walked down the path of 'happiness'
        and found no art along the way.
I realised that this path was a lie, made for me.
I walked down the path of art
        and found literature, history, blood,
        heavily dissected brains bleeding paint,
        strings of pearls in teacups,
        much needed self-expression,
        a rejection—nay, an anarchistic agenda
        against the crowd,
        against the easily devised, digested and disposed
        modernism; sought
        nature, and the magic of words;
And there found my happiness.

Girl with Goldfish

Under clothes, behind books,
Inside shoes, she looks.
In bins, diaries, fridge and sinks,
She looks in every place she thinks
        She could have put her goldfish.

Exhausted, curled up in a ball,
She hears a knocking on the wall.
Not the wall, she thought, instead
The knocking came from in her head;
        That funny, little goldfish!

Out of sight, but in her mind,
No wonder it was hard to find!
But no matter how she shook about,
She could not get that goldfish out:
        That stubborn, little goldfish!

So, she cried and cried to get it out,
Her tears like water from a spout;
She cried until her head ran dry,
Dry, and can't remember why
        she even cried at all…

Woolf Street

If only gentlefolk could haunt streets,
Unseen;
We are not afforded luxuries such as
        metaphorical pencils:
A real one clenched between our fingers
        offers greater protection.
It should not have to be this way:
I feel the tense, the terrified—
On that bridge, I expose my throat to myself
        and challenge my own vulnerabilities.

Inheritance

I do not wish to inherit money,
>but the sacred knowledge of my home;

How the wind knows when to whisper
>and when to roar...

The patience of the trees, standing tall,
>their branches like nurturing arms...

The gentle flow of the river,
>ever soft, ever moving...

The resilience of the ground,
>stable under the enormous weight
>of living...

To offer my body as shelter,
>to grow and provide,
>yet stand strong against the most violent
>of storms...

Appreciate all my mountains and hills,
>valleys and scars
>(like rings of growth on my hips)...

And to be like a waterfall;
>To fall is not the end,
>Find rainbows along the way,

And one day,
> You will eventually find yourself
> at the top of the waterfall again.

Last, but not least,
From the Sun and the Moon,
> I endeavour to keep moving,
> But always enjoy the view.

52

Sitting outside, in the moonlight,
Wondering what the life of a star's like;
A grey whale swims in a mirrored sea,
A lonely call, only heard by me.
Ocean cries, a cliff bows its head,
To hear the words the whale said.
As he breathes, a star explodes,
But his cry, no one knows.
Silent giant, swimming in stars,
Is it lonely where you are?
On this cliff, look down to see,
Maestro of solitude, far from me.
Lonely whale, are you cold?
No mate out there for you to hold?
Or do the stars protest
Against your own happiness?
They enjoy your warm and dulcet tone,
And want to keep you for their own.
Peripatetic; seek, without regret,
The other half of your duet,
For the stars that curse and flee
Shall not dim your scenery.

Glide throughout your universe,
Compose your song, chorus and verse,
And here I'll watch in admiration,
Your genius, your determination.

Ship of Theseus

All these boxes,
No matter their shape and size
Cannot hold me.
I move and change
Like water,
And all those boxes fall apart.
Not even dams, rivers and oceans
Can contain me.
Liquid; solid; gas;
I surpass all form
And move as I please.
No thought is the same as yesterday,
Neither is my body.
We rest, we repair,
New souls come and go;
I am changed, but remain.
      What is *me*?
We, ships of Theseus,
Pass each other by.

Ouroboros

Dawn consumes night with a slow, scarlet mouth,
And in the evening, dusk consumes day.
Ouroboros slides around the planet
In clouds and light, its head guided by the
Sun, as the Earth dances around its throne.
Celestial snakes of the sky, entwined,
Forever coiled in their gravity;
Seeking to devour each other, but
Only just catch the tail of their mate.
When did the Earth begin this mating dance?
Or did the Sun start this galaxy waltz?
Is it a dance of courtship, or a fight?
Perhaps the Moon desires to free us
From this engagement with the giant star.
But We are merely grains of sand, viewers
In the cosmic arena of planets,
Relying on stars and the ocean waves,
And the rise and fall of light, to see it
This is a dance of planets, or a fight.

Love-Lies-Bleeding

Listen close with ears unjaded
The forever-song of Love-Lies-Bleeding;
The weeping red, the Never-Fade,
A song, she sings, for one hundred years.

Her frozen heart is frozen still,
Although the snow has passed;
She stole her breath and her love,
Winter-bound is amaranth's hearth.

She welcomes not the seasons change,
To ruby pearls, she clutches close.
She holds her breath and waits
Until the ground is deathly white.

Then Winter comes, sees her rouge,
A stain within the snow,
Her beauty frozen, evermore,
The amaranth's love lies bleeding.

Soup

Warm tides through suffocating tunnels, I
Embrace with a loving mind the liquid
Blanket that envelops my cold insides.
Silky broth of savoury sensations,
A lingering scent of satisfaction,
A fountain of flavour, a warm retreat
That rejuvenates my tired hands
And thaws the heart of a numbing Winter.
A palatable potion, prepared with
The Sun and eaten with the Moon; a fire
Of the hearth burns within, melting every
Muscle of its pain and cold exhaustion.
Life returns to these fingers, and the dark
Night slips into waves of starlit oceans.

Ammil

When Winter walks in waves of white,
Weaves a blanket for those who sleep;
The Great Slumber, She watches over all
With waters, wait to wet their lips,
And guards the burrows buried deep.

She wanders, lonely, lovingly,
She barely sees the day;
Yet as we wake, and She departs,
Soft kisses she has left
On every blade of grass.

Innsæi

A raging storm in iris sea,
Red streams run thick with salt,
Crystalise, the corners cut, and
Let inner tides pursue.

The salt drags in me
A tidal ambition, breaks;
And iris storms look within
To rocking waves,
Flooding cavities of lung and bone,
Bringing air and marrow to war.

Tossing ships on heartstring lines,
And anchors stomach-deep,
Double beat of marching drums
Resonates in ribbed battlegrounds.

Side to side, it sways,
Determined, hands do shake.
The ocean's salt slides into me
In rivers clear,
Yet carrying ambition brewed.

The sea grows still and silent,
And salt settles, skin-deep;
An iris moon looks beyond
As a lighthouse, to watch for
Oncoming storms.

Revolution

Like an ever-turning key,
Or a trip around the Sun,
Life cycles like the Dewey decimal system:
Starts with the pursuit of advancement
        and religion,
And ends with war.

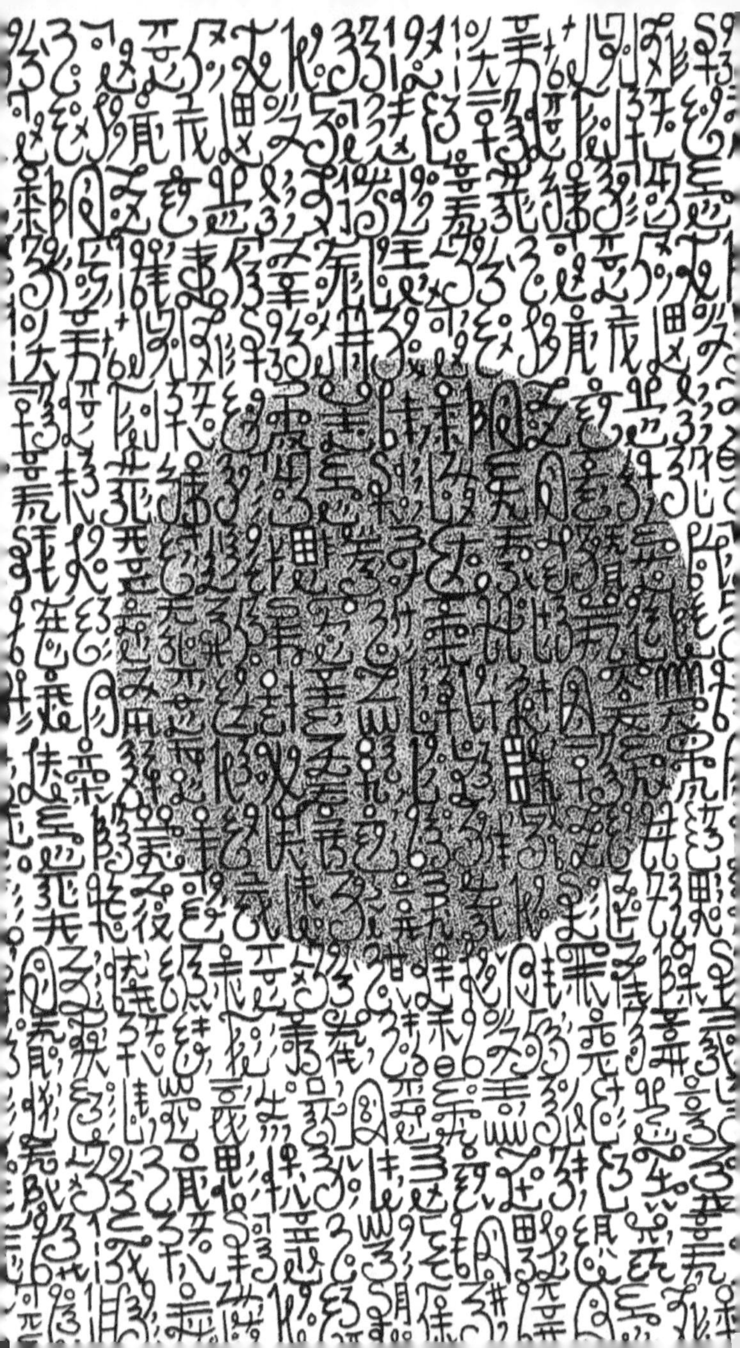

This Kingdom

This Kingdom is not ours;
Never was, never will be.
We are nothing but a soft-skinned foetus,
Barely formed, still blind to our surroundings,
Kicking away at our blue womb.
The rivers of our placenta are drying up now
And the blood moves slow,
        sluggish and stripped of any health.
This kingdom belongs to The Body,
For they are one and the same.
This kingdom has one God;
His hand has roamed every intimate inch of The Body,
        knows every crevice,
        every valley,
        every being,
        every secret.
We know him well; He knows us best.
In this kingdom, our God, Death
will meet us all,
Perhaps more than once.

www.ingramcontent.com/pod-product-compliance
Lightning Source LLC
Chambersburg PA
CBHW022016290426
44109CB00015B/1192